SLOUCHING THE DREAM

SLOUCHING THE DREAM

Poems

SPENCER BUTT

$|N_1|O_2|N_1|$

CANADA

*Publisher's note: This book is a work of fiction. Names, characters, places and
incidents are either the product of the author's imagination or are used
fictitiously, and any resemblance to actual persons living or dead
is entirely coincidental.*

Library and Archives Canada Cataloguing in Publication

Butt, Spencer, 1982–, author
Slouching the dream / Spencer Butt.

Poems.
ISBN 978–1–988098–09–8 (paperback)

I. Title.

PS8603.U866S56 2016   C811'.6   C2015–908443–1

Printed and bound in Canada on 100% recycled paper.

Now Or Never Publishing
#313, 1255 Seymour Street
Vancouver, British Columbia
Canada V6B 0H1

nonpublishing.com
Fighting Words.

We gratefully acknowledge the support of the Canada Council for the Arts
and the British Columbia Arts Council for our publishing program.

For Grampa for inspiring me and Stephanie for putting up with me.

The Lost City of YYZ

inside
up wide wooden winding stairs
we march towards the heavens with anxious legs
tired of the world below
drenched with the want to amelia earhart
in the name of escaping
          for the love of adventure

every floor a different business
with a cheap sign
chinese characters i can't read
no signs
on the top floor
no help
no maps
no guides to hold our hands
just a secret passed down to the lucky ones
a black door at the end of the hallway
dark as coal
a second smaller stair in its guts
and then a small wooden door
that looks like it ran away from an outhouse
prop that door open so you don't get locked out

then the roof top
the last tree fort in a scrapyard of dead robots and kaiju
you can see everything forever
          your eyeballs are the swirl of infinity

in that moment you are an uncontacted tribe hiding from
loggers in the amazon
the last of the neanderthals building a fire and worrying that
you shouldn't have

been so welcoming to your new neighbors
be afraid of lighting
make a good spear
the idea of climbing down has yet to be painted
on your hollow stone walls
   no elders pass down that story
down there is death
down there is devolution
down there is dirty and noisy and angry and everything
terrible that ends with a y
and up here is the cave the kids from *the goonies* wound up in
with no fratellis' and no deleted scene giant octopus
up here
   up here is our time
up here epic journeys go to die
just so that they can be reincarnated
and minds go to do white-out keg stands
and you can never stay too long
because you don't wanna be there
when the next ghost shows up
looking for a personal oasis
it's less special
when we're all special

Enduring Descendants of the Sasquatch

we ride to the very end of leslie spit
and we just call it the spit,
            because everybody does
i don't think most people even
know she has a first name

all of the roads are completely haunted
and my jeans are wet with sweat
the beads push through
the denim and rub noses with the pitch black
we have to stop half way
along the water front
            near the sugar plant
to take our jackets off and stuff them into our backpacks

the electric skyline looks far
but i wish it was further
i disconnect from my surroundings
as i take a photo of it
with my cell phone and make the photo look
like it's from the 70's,
because things that happened before i was born seem better
i catch myself ruining the magic,
            looking behind the curtain
i text my girlfriend and tell her
that i'm so excited that we
just moved in together

at the edge of the world
we see boats in the distance
drink beers that we fish out from underneath our coats
            the rotting lighthouse watches over us
                        a loving foster mother with the rotating
                        head of a bioluminescent owl

we try to throw increasingly larger and heavier chunks of
concrete
into the water
wonder what we'd do if something
threw them back at us
we talk about girls
and some of us are dying to talk about guys but can't think
of a segue
that doesn't give their stomach a third degree sunburn
we hang our empties on the gnarled ends
of the zombie rebar that's reaching out at us
it looks like a blue collar pagan shrine to an octopus god
too terrible to be named
the breeze smells like an unexpectedly big tax return
baseball hats are adjusted to let them brush up against our
foreheads
and you can't see any of our tattoos
and we don't need to say anything

we stop at an old abandoned bridge next to the don valley
on the way home
we climb over fences to stand on it and talk about people we
knew in high school
then we ride to another bridge
        north of there
that actually overlooks the highway
we lean our bikes up against the railing
we watch cars and wonder what it'd be like to be leaving the
city in such a late night hurry

i get ready for bed in the bathroom
so i don't wake her up when i get home
and when i crawl in next to her
          smelling like the dirt from a half drunk hourglass
she still rolls over to kiss me goodnight
and reverse sleeping beauty's me

JOB STOPPERS

at least they're not something really offensive
stupid i can deal with
        not even stupid
i think they're kind of clever and nice and pretty and accessible
is there such a thing as "an accessible hand tattoo"
is the world really moving towards that
i don't think i look like a bad guy

some old russian men came into the restaurant i work at
went off on me about how
where they come from only real criminals have hand tattoos
i told them that my knuckles say "read more" so i don't think
i'd last too long in
a russian prison
and they told me that i would definitely not last long
        (kind of a diss)
and that i was a fool for associating myself with such scum
such villainy
i just had to agree and walk away because i was on the clock
people who have a tendency to act like assholes have to realize
that when you act like a dickhead to someone who works
in the customer service industry
we always have to just stand there and nod
and if we weren't so desperate for a job they would get our
honest reactions
instead of the red hot sulk of our anorexic wallets

i don't see myself ever getting sick of these tattoos
but the older i get
        and the closer i edge to a "career"
                (whatever the hell that means)
my tattoos worry me more and more
and i hope that there are enough members of this tribe

that the bosses of the future will either have to accept us
  or just won't notice or care
  or think twice
so that i never really regret any of the entries i've made in
this scrap book

KNOWING

i know i shouldn't have gone to the doctor
expecting to hear that i was a diabetic
but it made it that much more awesome
        sweeter
when she said that i wasn't
and if it worries me that much
i could exercise more or eat less junk food
but fuck you because i love that stuff and nobody tells me
what to do
not you, not the doctor, not myself,
not the ads outside the gym i walk past on my way to work
        nobody
have you ever even had candy

so what if i stand sideways in front of the mirror
        every morning when i get dressed
        every night when i get undressed
trying to stand up as straight as possible
and i frownzamine my posture
scoop my gut
suck it in
        · flex where my muscles should be
sometimes i even make my pipe cleaner legs flex
i measure my hairline to a specific freckle i have on my
forehead to see if it's retreated any further
and look at how much of my body is covered in tattoos
and wish i had more of them to conceal these flaws
and imagine i had a bigger dick that was shaped like a
weapon
or a bird of prey
or god
or god's dick

so what
everybody does this
i hope

ONE IN A MILLION

if you don't put my poems in your magazine
it means
you are stupid and don't understand emotions
it means i'm the best writer in the world and everyone
around me is an idiot
it's the end of the world
we're all gonna die
nothing good will ever happen again
i'm gonna call in sick from work
so that i can cry and complain
reconsider everything i've ever done in my life
think that's it's all been a waste of time
shit, i'm already over thirty
i can't start over
i'll play video games all day instead of writing
    like i told myself i would
        like i told my girlfriend i would
then when she comes home and asks how the writing has
been going
i'll jettison the panic attacks i've been hoarding
because i had no choice but to do nothing all day
    to feel sorry for myself all day
        to overreact all day
i'll tell her i couldn't
think of anything deep and cool and important to write about
i'll act like the world doesn't understand me
because i'm such a unique individual
    oh really
    how many other guys out there
    do you see with beards and tattoos
    who wear tight
        because i'm getting fat
    all black clothes

who listen to heavy metal and

who like comic books and science fiction and horror and write poetry

the answer is none because i am a wonderful snowflake of sorrow when really i'm just a lazy sad sack who's terrified of being rejected again

Note to Self

i don't love nothin like i love you
don't feel nothing but you
got you only skin
got achin' nerves
got soft brown hairs on my arms a reachin' for ya
got wet cement fingertips waiting for you to scratch your
name in them with a stick
got you taste buds
and you words use my lips like a hammock for you

gonna get mature with you
gonna figure things out with you
gonna have babies with you and me features
baby's gonna have a big head cuz we both got big heads
baby's gonna have you eyes and you tiny little mouth
baby's gonna have no attention span cuz of me
gonna have us bad irish and german tempers
gonna go bald(er) and grey with you
gonna have thicker glasses with you

please never get amnesia
don't have alzheimer's or dementia when we get slower and
run through calendars
i can't bear you lookin at me like a stranger
we just watched that sad movie about that
that i didn't want to watch and i cried more than i wanted to
and drowned in the bathtub of my dumb heavy eyelids

These ARE My Cool Clothes

the first time i try to hold my daughters hand in public
and she refuses because she thinks it's embarrassing
i think it'll kill me
i think it'll kill me to go to work today too
i think it will kill me to go to a party where i don't know a
lot of people
i think it'll kill me if i'm hanging out with my girlfriend and
her pals
 and she walks away
leaving me to fend for myself as she takes a pee or gets
another drink or meets somebody better
i think it'll kill me if i put my insecurities under
a magnifying glass
the sun burning a hole through my worry
a budding psycho aiming a solar powered death ray at an ant
colony
i think it'll kill me to dress nicer
i think it means i'm selling out
but what i know it means is that i'm afraid of getting older
i think it'll kill me to not eat a box of donuts a day
i think it'll kill me if i don't get in at least an hour of video
games a day
i think it'll kill me to be happy with what i have
to be happy with where i am
i think it means i'm giving up
what do i have left to strive for
if i don't have these cool goth feelings
and this awesome depressed face
 then what do i have going for me
what did i buy all of these black clothes for
i think it'll kill me to listen to less misanthropic music
the brooding nurtures me
i think it'll kill me when i realize that a brooding thirty-two

year-old man is an asshole
or a batman
i think it'll kill me to get into better shape
i think it'll kill me not to as well
but i think it'll kill me more to do something slightly un-fun
for an hour a couple times of week
i think the fact that i get out of breath bending over to tie
my shoes will kill me
and i think it'll kill me to think about that too much

if my wife ever leaves me
i think it'll kill me
i think of her opinion of me and i think that if she ever
thought i was a loser
    or a disappointment it would kill me
i think water where i can't see the bottom will kill me
i think the things that live in the darkness of that water exist
only to kill me
i think it'll kill me to try harder
i think rejection will kill me and the best defense for that is a
total lack of offense
i think it'll kill me to admit that i'm wrong about something
even if i realize i'm wrong part way through the argument
i think it would kill me to urn into somebody
that i never wanted to be
i think it'll kill me when my mom dies
i thought seeing my grampa on his deathbed would kill me
it killed me even more when he died and i didn't say goodbye
i think it would kill me if anything bad ever happened to my
little sister
so many bad things have happened to my little sister and i
think it would kill me to ever have to go through any of
those personally

it would kill me if she stopped trying because he if she can't
take something
i can't take anything

i think it'll kill me if don't get dumb tattoos as often as
some people take vitamins
what else am i supposed to hide underneath
i think it'll kill me to live without camouflage and peacock
arms
i think pornography and shopping will kill me
i think it would kill me if we proved conclusively the yeti
wasn't real
because living in a world of maybes
is better than living in a world of definitely nots

CAREER OPPORTUNITIES

when i was a kid
really little
dink the clown little
i wanted to be a paleontologist because i thought dinosaurs
were incredible
they were so much bigger and badder
than the jabronis in cages at the zoo
but when i saw andre the giant for the first time
i realized that maybe my talents would be better spent
learning how to leg drop shit

i remember one day my granny and grampa found a box of
those old rubber wrestling figures
on the side of the road and gave them to me
i remember the level of insanity that instantly overcame me
in some weird hp lovecraft
seeing the elder gods in real life sort of way
soon i had a pretty good roster going for me
i even had a miss elizabeth figure to escort my macho man
figure down to the ring
a mean gene okerlund figure to let the crowd know
which titans would be clashing that night
i used my *he-man* and *marshall bravestar* action figures as
jobbers to help put my other action figures over

eventually i reached that phase in ones life
when toys lose their magic
and the homoeroticism of rasslin' was too much for my
spontaneous boner getting welcome to puberty body
i gave them all away to the second hand store
run by the local cottage hospital

      i felt like el hijo del santo
strolling down the streets
without his silver mask for the first time
      just a regular dude with an abnormally barreled chest
as an adult nerd i regret that
as much as sting probably regrets choosing
tna over the wwf

when i was in my late teens
the wcw got me back into wrestling
part of that stems from the fact that
by that point in my rural ontario life
i realized that no matter what i did i would never be
considered cool
so fuck it who cares let's party
i would make vhs compilations of all the cruiserweights
started wearing cut-off jean shorts non-stop in the summer
because that's what billy kidman wore
he could do a shooting star press that was so clean
it was a fuck you to the laws of physics
thought about him whenever i tried doing flips
into the pond behind the golf course
i remember seeing ultimo dragon for the first time
and wanting to move to japan so bad
i loved all the luchadores
felt a strange level of comradery with them
because i was in french immersion and
french is sort like spanish
so, you know,
kindred spirits
      relatability is a hell of a drug

when i was in my late twenty's i went to san francisco and
bought a la parka mask from some guy on the street
       in this mexican neighborhood
then i drank short cans of *tecate*
and wore it in my hotel room that night
while eating american only flavours of ben and jerry's ice
cream in my boxers
as i watched lord of the rings on cable tv
       by myself
and the level of sheer contentment was paralyzing

If I Ever Disappear

hi
welcome to the mid-life crisis
help phone line/sex party chat
toronto's most erotically depressing
1-800 number
when you're ready to begin
          please press pound to exhale violently

press one if you'd like to
be an expert at something
but don't want to practice anything until you're
actually good at it
i wish i played guitar
i wish i played piano
i wish i spoke 10 different languages
i wish i could breakdance
i wish i had a black belt in judo

press two
if you think your crooked teeth give you character
but are worried they'll continue moshing
and eventually puncture your skull like a narwhal
or
turn you into an ugly cartoon
press two
if you're worried that one day you'll go
from quirky to meth head
and you think about french kissing people
          how their tongue would recoil
in horror
when it rubs up against
the mine field
in your mouth

press three
if you love it when life
simultaneously
synchs up with the music in your headphones
and you head nod accordingly
and start picturing a music video
but when you try to have sex while music is playing in the
background
you try too hard to match the rhythm
        and you do not really have any rhythm
you get distracted
        it kills your buzz
you and your partner
get into a sad argument
that revolves around your feelings of self worth

press four
if you regret never having really long hair
that you can part in the middle
and have both ends hang in braids
before you went bald
        i mean started shaving your head
        for no reason
        just because you felt like it
        and you're still young and cool and attractive

press five
if you've ever woken up crying

press six
if you think you would
        given the chance

choose to live forever
so that you could see what
life is like 500 years from now
and space
and aliens
and robots
and advancements in technology

press seven
when you realize that means you'll see all of your loved ones
die
and how the thought of your significant other growing older
without you
turns your insides
        into a mom losing sight of her toddler
        in a crowded mall

press eight
to be connected with other people
in your area
        hot singles
your age
who don't think that they have their shit together
but who you think are totally on the right track
        these bonding experiences may be recorded for
training purposes

press nine
if waking up is stressful
if the clouds passing over you look
like a friend tapping their watch
as you arrive late for something

a movie
            dinner
when they really need you
       and you don't realize it
continue pressing nine
to offer a guilty smile
       that does nothing to mend their hurt feelings
to you it's that you should have left 5 minutes earlier
but you were
dicking around with your phone
       to them it's a sense of under-appreciation
or un-reciprocated friendship
that can hollow bones
and make your teeth wince
press nine
repeatedly
       as fast as you can
            pretend you're playing street fighter and you
suck at it
finger tapping frantically
your finger is that girl who's dangling foot bobs wildly when
she crosses her legs
keep doing that
do it as a distraction
       pair it with blurred vision
as you think about your life choices
and mistakes and missed opportunities
press nine as much as you like
but know
       by this point
that you're pressing nine
just for you

press zero
to repeat these options
or have more options
       to keep grasping
keep dropping your feelings
on the ground
       a bread trail
seeking to lead like-minded individuals into a hand shake
hug
press zero
to reboot the system
press zero
if your brain shuts down after being
in most social situations for too long
press zero
if you have x amount of pre-programmed responses
       a finite amount of ring tones to use as conversation
pieces
and when you run out
you don't know what to do
you feel lost
get tired
get sad
get quiet
press zero for a service inspection
       press zero for a software update to your personality
press zero
with the precision of a metronome
so that the pulsing
mimics a heartbeat

mash all buttons
if you wish this wasn't all so relevant
or
feel free to
hang up and explode

I Ain't Never Did Nothin' To Nobody

the words
            i didn't do shit
fell out of his mouth
dried out spit that could be cum
hit the bouncer's windshield
and was batted away by a white knuckled wiper
            it's true,
he didn't do a damn thing
didn't think before a winter's worth of snow
disappeared up his nostril
and he pretended the nosebleeds
were a casualty of the dry weather

didn't do anything when he should have been thinking
that flinging an empty tumbler over his shoulder
on a crowded dance floor
was a bad idea

didn't think to say sorry
when it kissed
the blond girl with the cute, green shoes on the face;
her forehead erupting with a stop sign
            the stop sign running,
mixing with sweat and hairspray and stinging shocked eyes
kept white by black light

outside
my efforts to calm things down
were merely the daydreams
lost in the wandering eye of a hurricane
another drunk asshole
wanted to be a knight in shining armor;
            a superhero in perfectly cuffed jeans and a store

bought haircut
i thought i had defused the bomb
when he came charging down the sidewalk
alpha freight train to the rescue

fists fell
and the impact
made the same sound as a firm
pat on the back

Be Good/Have Fun

i love my mom so much
and every time she doesn't answer her phone
i worry that she's dead and her cats
                              they're like your little brothers
are eating her
and i hate it and i wish she would always answer
and please never die
and my little brothers would never eat your still warm body
and why am i even giving that statement so much thought

i know you're getting older
          grayer
your face has more wrinkles now than it did when i was a
little kid
and thought you were so tall for a mom and now
you don't even come up to my shoulder
          you're a tiny pixie mom
who dresses nice and has a nice face and a nice smile and a
nice way about you
and i wish you'd find a nice man
          in real life
          on the internet
and he was good to you
and i liked him
and my little sister liked him
and you guys could grow old together
and move out of your little apartment
          that always kind of smells like my little brothers' litter
box
and you went out a little more
and saw how great you are
because that's all i see when i look at you
          or photos of you

or picture you in my head
and i know you don't need a man to be happy
and i'm cool if you're cool
i just hope you're cool all the time
and you're not lonely in the suburbs
          watching your shows
                    smoking weed with my little brothers
and sometimes going to the casino with your girlfriend ronnie
you guys should be gay and take care of each other
and make sure you're both always cool
and i'm so proud of you for booking a trip to vegas together
cuz it's better than the
shitty casinos in ontario canada
and i'm so proud of you for being such a good single mom
when we were younger
          i'm so proud and thankful
and i should make more of an effort to take the bus north to
you
and you like going to the chinese buffet when i come up
because when we were kids and didn't have a lot of money
it felt like the richest thing in the world to eat as much as
you want
and you love hearing about what i'm up to
and always ask if i have any shows coming up and
          are they on weekends
so you can stay out late
and maybe have a drink before taking public transit back
home because
you won't drive at night
or on highways or in the city even though buses take forever
and you listen to your little ipod we got you
and probable do little mom dances with your little hands and

little feet
and you always come to see my stupid too loud bands play
and you're a good mom
and your mom and dad were the best grandparents i could
have ever hoped for
and i wish they weren't dead so fucking much
and i'm gonna be good like you
when i have little monsters that think r's are w's
but you need to answer that god damn phone a little more
ok

WRK

this job hates me
        this job wouldn't make me feel so shitty if it didn't
i'm nothing but nice to this job
but when this job is done with me it always sneaks out while
i'm still sleeping
        this job
wears too much cologne and i reek of it when i come home
and my girlfriend makes me shower before i can get close to
her
this job is full of work friends that you only text to see if
they can switch shifts
that you drink with at staff parties but don't go out of your
way to say hi to
when you see outside of this job
this job will break your heart without a second thought and
get a brand new you
this job is too easy
i'm too comfortable around this job
this job is a labyrinth of cubicles and angry customers
who take the frustrations of their garbage lives out on you as
you smile politely
because they know you can't respond how you'd like to
because this job is always watching you
this job eats days
this job never lets me do what i want to do
i'm worried this job will be the death of me
that i'll be old and pathetic and sad and make other people sad
        this job will make an example out of me
there is a strict ban on ambition at this job
i blame so much on this job
i used to adore this job
was so stoked to have this job
tried to get my friends to work here

i still count myself lucky to have a job like this
but i need more than this job
this job is just fine
this job is your high school punk band playing to
two hundred kids at a rec center in the suburbs
great
now what else
what more
what's next
this job is no magic eight ball
this job is a golden calf disguised
as a mechanical fortuneteller
and if you're not careful it'll age you over night
it wont be long before we start swallowing our watches in
an attempt at acquiring a taste for time travel

It's Still Real To Me, Dammit

bobby heenan's brain is my favorite move in all of wrestling
it killed me the first time i saw
photos of him after he lost his jaw to cancer
now he looks like a sad sock puppet
he was never overly fit but he's too skinny all over now
looks like he should have died
i mean
i'm glad he didn't
but i came up with a cool tribute tattoo that i'm going to
get when
he finally does get thrown over the top ropes of god's terrible
royal rumble
so the selfishness coursing through my bones
keeps checking the grim reaper's countdown
while he plays cards with mike awesome
eddie guerrero and chris kanyon

my grampa
          who i looked up to more than my father,
used to talk about how great classy freddie blassie was
he went down for the eternal three count shortly after my
grampa died
and all the emotions i had kept bottled up
sealed tight like paul bearer's urn
turned into entrance pyrotechnics
i cried a lot when the wwe played a tribute to him before
raw that week
set to the tune of some shitty evanescence song
i felt so white trash and lonely
broken like syd's leg and droz's neck
sitting by myself in my room
in my 20's crying over nu metal and pro wrestling
as tears ambushed the trailer park that lives in my cheekbones
thinking about the guy that taught me how to fish

PLEASE HANG UP AND TRY YOUR CALL AGAIN

a while ago
    when looking through a photo album of my baby pictures
my old man started bragging to me about how he used to
use me
to help him pick up women
while my mom
would be at home
    thinking he was doing a nice thing for her and enjoying
her day off
they're divorced now

he passed this information off to me
through his tiny jaundicing
    porcelain tombstones
lips curled up into an assholes horseshoe
eyes that gleamed
    you're welcome
as if he had just passed off some golden nugget of knowledge
that would only aid in accelerating
my inevitable metamorphosis
into a fully blown scumbag
my destiny was now sealed
displayed like the small faded square photo of
two year old me in over sized sunglasses
    gripping an empty beer bottle
underneath the transparent cellophane layer of memory sealant

my guts went garbage
    as if the arrival of my sister and i hadn't done enough
damage already
our birth effectively grassy knolled my mom's dreams of
becoming a stewardess
and rerouted her potential to part time work in a phone

book factory
making both the 3rd of december, 1982
and october 13th, 1984
horribly wrong numbers for her

my sister and i often speak of how
mom's life would have been much better had we never been
born
but my hands are way too rural to ever grasp a concept like
time travel
    shaky even with a pen
fingers fumbling through the alphabet like a drunk fighting
with his car keys

and there's no point in writing
    sorry i didn't miscarriage
over and over again until the ink runs out like somebody
yelled
    gun
instead
i'm left sitting across from my old man at the dining room
table
still trying to process exactly
what the fuck just happened
like i'm strapped into the electric chair
damp sponge on my head
waiting for the switch to fall
and the power goes out

i know he could feel the disappointment
radiating from my silence
but my old man just keeps turning the pages of the scrapbook
with this all too familiar hodgepodge of

annoyance
frustration and genuine surprise wrinkling across his face
as the high five he had hoped for
gets lost in translation

How to Pluck and Cook a Swan

i didn't wanna hit him
and then when i did
i didn't wanna stop hitting him
the violence was so addictive
my junkie fists crashing on the couch of his cheekbone
or maybe i wasn't hooked
just thought i looked cool with the cigarette in my mouth
and my first reactions can be terrifying
and i went from 6'4" of gentle giant to 240lbs of bad intentions
as fast as my fingers could popple
vision warm and fuzzy
and even after his eyes spun
tried watching his back
tried looking for the fire exit
tried desperately to shift the actions of a total asshole into
reverse
did summersaults of regret
knuckles kept meeting his face
            excitedly
                        like each time was the first time
my fists have no short-term memory
my elbow was a yoyo string with a lighting bolt at the end
fuses blew under pressure
and the blackout threw a burlap sack
over what happens when you don't stop beating someone

and i barely remember getting up
            or walking over
            or knocking him onto his back
i can kind of picture his personal belongings
yard-sailing through the uncut grass in the park
or the look of surprise when
somebody finally answered the call

that everybody tried to ignore
until the ringing in everybody's ear became unbearable
but i remember being tackled and pulled off and
turning and realizing
that it was a friend who knew that
        i can quit anytime i want to
is usually a dying man's cry for help
and my girlfriend
who moments before had been recoiling nervously
from the booze soaked venom of this brain-dead cobra
told me i had to calm down
said she was glad i was there
pushed me back and away from ground zero
with her hands on my chest
her friend held up her french bulldog in my face to distract
my line of sight
its oversized dummy grin and attention hog lipstick dick
faded the red in my windows to a dull easter pink
my right hand hurt for days

Fast Fold

i'm envious of it all
the relaxed attitudes
good sleeps
you look nice in clothes
i look nice in the dark
i don't even look that nice in the dark
i look nice with your eyes closed

i'm envious of the haircuts
the beards
the timing
the foresight
the laissez-faire
deep breaths
the achievements
the natural confidence

i'm envious of the money
the food
the flexibility and the muscle tone
the jobs
the freedoms
the structure
support and stability

i'm envious of the dead
people who live for today
people who plan for tomorrow
people who haven't already peaked
the warmth
the chill that reminds you of the warmth
the grip
the velcro
sure footedness

i'm envious of the painless
the comfort
the focus
the nothingness
the bright light
the adrenaline
the rush and the silence

i'm envious
and i will be
for good
for better or for worse
the long haul
the road trip
the always
the end

Ticker Tape Aloha

this consciousness is a wildfire
we're surrounded by coincidence
acting like a universal cosmic tech-support
        and we feel lighter everyday
we tie ourselves down with dead end jobs
mouths sewn shut with braces like chain link fences
strapped to medical gurneys
the straightjackets feel like *snuggies*

lumbering with heavy armageddons and tedious lungs
these fleece nooses keep my throat calm
like wrapping kids with autism in blankets
the overwhelming pressure makes ocean sounds
        as our auras hiss white noise
these quantum tongue twisters and astral projectionists
centering my chi
through death metal
as i meditate in the bathtub surrounded
by lavender bubble bath
feeling totally crazy and afraid to talk to a shrink
because if science confirms it
then things get too serious
too real
the seatbelt of fiction is keeping me alive

things get louder the more tired you are
the closer to sleep you inch
forcing yourself to stay awake
watching tv and continually turning the volume down
and you wake up with the television nearly on mute

feel free to steal parts of this for use as a suicide note
since you're willing to put in the work for something that
i keep calling in sick to

Psychic Fanfare

in ten years
i'll be on the verge of celebrating a decade
of being married to the best human being i've ever met in
my entire stupid life
in ten years we'll have two kids
a son and then a daughter
      in that order
            (it has to be in that order)
and they will be healthy and smart and funny
and kind and great

in ten years we won't be renting
in ten years we'll be home owners
maybe not in this city
but somewhere
and it'll be the best
in ten years i'll have a lawn to cut and a driveway to shovel
in ten years i won't think i need to live in a city
where i can walk to a heavy metal concert every night
i'll start thinking about how cool it is that my kids have a
creek to swim in and a yard to build forts in
in ten years i'll feel better about my job
because in ten years i'll feel better about my life

in ten years i'll have at least two books published
and i'll swear less in my writing
i'll be more optimistic
in ten years i'll be more relatable
and likable
in ten years i still won't have written a best seller
but in ten years i'll measure success differently

in ten years i'll have a hologram
that projects from my belly button and tells me when i'm
hungry
right now i never know when i'm hungry
i just eat when i'm bored
or when i want to taste something good
and stop when i feel sick or have to go to the bathroom
in ten years i won't need to shave my head anymore
to try and hide the fact that i'm balding
time and genetics will permanently clear it
      like a brush fire
in ten years my beard will be grey and that will mask the
patchiness of it all
i'll tell myself i look like odin
      other people will tell themselves that i look like a
sketchy mall santa
in ten years i'll have more wrinkles
and less hearing and vision
in five years science will create a machine that you can
plug yourself into when you feel depressed
and it will fix you and you'll feel better about things
in ten years i won't need it anymore

in ten years
my kids will still have their grandparents
      all of them
in ten years we'll drive hover cars to family reunions
or be shot through tubes
or teleport
we'll talk about the people living on mars
and how life-like our robot co-workers are
and some new cult and some new tragedy and some new

snack food
in ten years i'll still be out of shape but
i'll stop sucking in my gut around girls with cool butts and
dudes with strong backs
            i will be more comfortable in my own skin
in ten years i'll have more dumb tattoos to use as both a
shield and force field
in ten years my brain will still think
the best time to mainline stress
is one in the morning
in ten years a couple of people i really love will probably be
dead and most of this will never happen

in ten years i'll still smile every time i look at my wife
still feel lucky
still feel excited when she's near me
in ten years we'll be planning the tenth birthday
surprise trip to *disney world* for our son
and i will have seen a dozen more movies about superheroes
and space wizards
and played a hundred new video games and read a hundred
more comic books
and i'll have about the same amount of friends
and i'll probably have owned at least one dog
and i'll stop always thinking about what could be better
down the road
and start thinking about how awesome tomorrow is
going to be
in ten years the bullshit of today
will be relegated to footnotes that
nobody bothers to read because
the rest of the story is too good

SLOUCHING THE DREAM

this makes sense
i just turned thirty and this makes sense
i'm starving to death
with ribs that stand out like a new family in a small town
so this makes sense
my halo and light bulb combo
have been hate fucking
and the light bulb has given birth to a
bouncing baby bald spot
so this makes sense
i'm out of shape and can't touch my toes
but if my posture keeps going the way it's headed
i'll be able to rest my chin on them
so this makes sense
the path i walk in life has no interest in coming full circle
refuses to make the journey redundant
so being a lantern fish
in the ink black guts of the dull grey ocean of toronto
makes sense
it would make sense to say that i've failed if my death is but
an echo of my birth

i will not die naked and helpless
i will rot with a satisfied grin on what's left of my face
as maggots make love to the unfinished books in my tiny
prune brain
my instincts are a doorstop
so it makes sense
the talking heads whisper from my stereo that
          we're on a road to nowhere
and i shrug and nod   .

we exist in billboards and twenty second sound bites
so it makes sense
and the lack of focus and compasses that do bermuda triangle
windmills
are the coat of arms of a new generation
so this makes sense
you can be anything you want to be overwhelms us
the voice of reason is hoarse
          is swallowing glass
you are everything and nothing makes sense
you're getting too old for this shit makes sense
          you're dying to live and too old to die young
this crushes your breaths it makes so much sense
this terrible orgasm of fear
makes a sickening amount of sense
hands and knees quake
and ice cold aspirin blood
and eyes glued to our high school yearbooks

and we try to deny this makes sense
and wish it didn't make so much sense
and trying to explain why this makes sense
why we're ok with coursing through the unknown
with eyes tied back
will only result in your tongue tasting like the lunatics we
give a wide birth to on the sidewalk
we're mummifying ourselves in the safety of believing that
everybody else is this lost
that the fringe is still soft
that we're happy no matter what
we're embracing the daily decay
and colour coordinating with the rust

life is in a perpetual state of exhaustion
our brains never shut up
so we try to take the batteries out
treat them like over-sensitive smoke detectors
this is the dawning of a new error

ALL OF THIS

i'd be more productive if i had a nicer pen
i'd be more productive if i had a better notebook
i'd be more productive if i got a laptop
    but it has to be silver and have an apple on the top
or my writing will be total bullshit
i'd be more productive if i had a better café to write in this
café used to be a lot better for art stuff but then it changed for
the worse because everybody realized how good it is and now
everybody except for me is a psychic vampire
or wasn't cool last week but is now very cool and i hate it
i'd be more productive if i wrote at the public library
    not that library
        this library
you're an idiot if you thought i meant that library
look at how this library looks compared to that one
god you're stupid for thinking what you thought

oh great
someone's sitting at the window seat that i want to sit at
and write at
    amazing
there goes another day's worth of productivity because
that guy is selfish and doesn't understand
my needs because he doesn't know me
i hate that guy
i've never seen him before in my life
but now i'm seeing him and how comfortable
he's pretending to be in my spot and
i absolutely hate him
i'd be a lot more productive if that guy would go fuck himself
i'd be more productive if i did cool drugs
    oh really
    you've done this drug before

i guess it's for losers now
that drug used to make me a genius
but if i did it now i'd just be some sell-out copywriter
i bet i'd be more productive if i took a picture of me being
productive
and put it on the internet
    why is no one "liking" how good i am at staying on task
i'd be more productive if i had more muscles
so i better stop what i'm doing and do push ups for less than
a minute
i should wear more productive clothes
god these pants are hard to make art in
i'd be more productive if i was sadder
if i had more problems in my life
i have to remember to be more self-destructive
what was thinking when i told my girlfriend that i loved her
so much
    honesty is suicide
      love is a crowbar to the face

To Make a Better Map

i forgot how to live
not forever
just temporarily
just now
i'm trying to remember again
hope it all comes swiveling back
these alarm clocks in bike spokes
this wasting time stings
this dust collected hates me
these feelings of
i should be doing more
and feeling like you don't know how

i forgot how to live
was stuck in my own throat
i choked
coughed out cartoon anvils and safes and pianos
that made effort paint splash and then accordion
my knees hurt
my back hurts
my brain barfs on the floor
at a house party and everybody goes
        fuck that guy

i forgot how to live
without being such a fucking baby
i forgot how to live without worry
without overanalyzing the void
        stare too close at the infinite blackness
        and your eyes go inkwell
i forgot how to live without
things that taste like other things
without the escape pod of role playing games

without dread and posturing
without skinheaded old times
without constant erections
without a constant parade of pretty women to make me feel
better about myself

i forgot
and now the memories come back through cracks in the
plaster
drafts let the light in
      being swallowed by whiteness
is more disorienting than baby steps with your eyes burnt out
as you try to sneak out of the bedroom to take a piss in the
middle of the night
without waking the person sleeping next to you

and i remember the meteorite hitting
      i remember absolutely nothing
          right before everything all at once
and i'm looking to settle down
somewhere dead center
and i'm taking a lot of pictures
in case i forget that i figured it all out

FROM THE GUT

i can't believe how fast this is all moving
       moving in the right direction
              but it's still moving at a good clip
and i wanted it to move this fast
but did not expect it to move so fast
i'm both glad and overwhelmed that it is moving so fast

i know that this is all good and will work out
       i know this and repeat it like a mantra or a parrot
a skipping record
a nervous tick
but i still get white knuckles and break a sweat
like when you first start learning to drive and you leave
your neighborhood street for the first time and
merge with cars that have somewhere to be
i have somewhere to be now
       i have someone to be now

this moves with the beautiful choreography of dean malenko
such dangerous precision
and a stone cold expression
so as not to reveal the baseline of panic
i'm always worried that one wrong move could jenga the
whole operation
       everything falls apart
          just ask hüsker dü

i'm not sure when i'll ever be comfortable
with the movement
i get motion sickness
when i think as far ahead as setting my dvr to record
a television program
that i wont be home for
but if this ever stops moving i'll die

Do More

closer to the light
up early and lie there and look at her
she sleeps with a heavy tongue
          her mouth is just a little open
she doesn't move much
and she'd call me a creep if she knew i was watching her
little face muscles twitch
she'd tell me to knock it off
and i'm crazy about her

my legs are restless and my mind is always more awake than
the rest of its shell
they pace like expectant fathers do in movies
treadmilling outside of the birthing room
my brain thinks it'll never wake up if i lie back down
          my brain has seen *the elephant man* too many times
i shimmy down to the foot of the bed because my side is
pressed tight to the wall and the window
and i get out and cartoon villain xylophone tip toe to the
living room
to kill things in videogames until she gets up and makes me
be less of a c.h.u.d.

i take all of the time ever to make instant pancakes
and they're still burnt or too skinny and look like crepes
we both acknowledge that we should have eaten out
but it's our only day off
          and getting dressed is for suckers

MURDERURRR

these motorized teeth click
i can't relax even when i'm unconscious
soak through bed sheets
the backs of my hands look like
a mad-fold-in of the shroud of turin
when i face-palm embarrassment
    when i peek-a-boo lip readers
    when i cradle campfire cheeks
        with gentle scoops of cold water from bathroom sinks
        and take deep breaths

this cross-walk under my wrists
    this flat-tire cripple thump under my earlobe
is a primary school teacher turning the lights on and off
so rapidly that little kids move like robots

we're flightless birds cursing airplanes
with drugs on our breath
and plastic gems for tears
and dream catcher sanitary napkins
we dry hump track marks
and o.d. on diet coke and buckets of fried chicken
our support groups meet to play dungeons and dragons
we have secret handshakes that twist fingers
into the darkest of the hillside thickets and rosary beads in
tornadoes

i love you with brass knuckle death row guilt
    hearts in and out
play it cool with smooth jazz small talk
    hearts in and out
and feign an acceptance of friendship with high fives
that linger to six
i stay positive by surrounding myself with good people

it's not a coincidence that all of my loved ones are doing
really great things
    that those i hold close radiate dangerous levels of potential
and my hair falls out
and the cancer sells all of its pieces at the art opening
and gets drunk and makes fuck on an empty
late night subway car on the way home
    my marrow vibrates with pride
neon yellow of my day

channel all of this
    every of this
wonder if any of this will come out as anything other than
pretentious abstract graffiti and whiny diary entries
    but what if the audience doesn't get it
        then you're doing it for the wrong people
we're not trying to be different
this is just what our tongues are shaped like
    what gets our eyes hard
until out fingers shoot emergency miracles
until stanzas hide under bright nuclear white televangelist suits
with marshmallow riot shield smiles
they touch our forehead
their life line cradling our worry
god's love tea bagging us
    into zen
feel the third rail of your chakra
itching to burst from the cocoon of your coolest outfit
writhe with awe inducing wonder
like an epileptic at a b-boy battle
my dream job is lottery winner but i won't buy tickets
because the lottery is for chumps
and i'm out of ideas

i will tongue kiss your ouija board curser until you move me
until you prove that i'm nuts
until i find the hidden cameras and i realize this was all an
elaborate set-up
my guardian angel isn't dead yet
my spirit animal is extinct
        is rabid
has yet to be discovered but i'm sure it exists
        it has to exist
is the orang pendek
is adjusting the rabbit ears on the roof of the vatican
        in a search for radio signals from outer space
is my haunted apartment
and when it feels neglected i hear phantom fingers snapping
and i welcome the terrifying diabetic numbness
of sleep paralysis
with rigid arms and old hag suspended animation hallelujahs

FIREWALLS

(*this poem was written using only subject headers from the Toronto Craigslist Missed Connections*)

Do you ever wonder
If A Guy Misses You
Value Village Queen
you jumping into store from elevator in First canadian place
elevator at drug store (midland and finch)
When a guy...
thinking of you
Shared Parenting
Oh, man...
Are you Filipino?
Hey sparky...was that you?
asian guy – winners – calvin klein thongs
what kind of woman i'm lookin for?
Big Stacks...
Black women at Walmart
You work at arby's in the eaton centre
Mc Donalds Bayview/Eglington
Yvonne, or Yvette, from Burger King
Starbucks, rainy afternoon
Israeli triathalon swim practice
I amputated part of my right middle finger tonight at a bar
in EY

YOU LIVE IN MY BUILDING
Indian Medicine Shows should come with mittens
your norwegian readhead santa might grant you a wish
Do you ever wonder...
Why her, why now
two peas in a pod
Westbound Queen streetcar in the early morning
A: I still miss you.

Ok, you win :)
Pretty woman down the street
I laughed at you last night
Chuck E Cheese
don't open
Woodys, sat. night, you were touching my ass
If you can read this, you found a wireless connection
To all the beautiful women I saw downtown today
tall blonde – legs like a mountain
nerdy guy in little italy
what was i thinking
snow in the village?

I ALWAYS WISH.. I was someone's missed connection..
hey snuggles, it's me..
you're my professor and I can't stop...
I'm your boss... but it's not awkward...
rainy nights, and where are you?
Rainy nights, and where are you?
I miss fisting you
to the man...
I made the wrong choice
where are you my pakistani sweet heart
My Aunt Flo Came To Visit
You fell asleep, I laughed...
Don't think twice, it's alright
It's time to move along.
you were panhandling?
Taco Bell Friday night – Brittania/Creditview
Sexy Cougar in Upper Canada Mall
to the good lord

juicy pink?
beatiful tv
Dammit!!
Has Anyone Missed Me?
Old Pervert On College Street Car...

CROATIAN ZORO AT WOODY'S
I got a haircut and you stole my heart on Lakeshore
attractive girl with cheese
Oh sweet one
I gave you gatorade

SCREEMERS- PIZZA PIZZA employee w/ long hair..listening to metal music
looking and looking and looking
I like you way to much
young lady in black stockings who got off at Christie
Price Choppers Model
I seen you at starbucks
We should've got married
Still skips a beat
you, even still.
To the girl who was grinding and spanking me at the Ween show
You won the dance contest...
2 girls making out on subway
surreal but nice
you again.
lets do this
You and I need to talk...
Computer says "no"

THE HAMMER

my mom's heart wasn't built for this world
i sat furiously in the back of a cab with thunderstorm eyes
as my sister lost her mind over the phone
and my girlfriend sat next to me rubbing my arm
the cab driver couldn't move fast enough no matter what
speed he was going
i wanted to hit something so hard that my own body
shattered like a frozen t-1000

coming back from a weekend of shopping
in beautiful buffalo new york
with her pals
my mom's heart said eat shit and went on strike
the ambulance picked her up from a *wendy's* parking lot as
her
girlfriends walked back and forth and considered whether or
not they had time
to run in and grab a frosty for the road

my mom doesn't have a cellphone
but she borrowed her friend's
        called my sister mid heart attack
        and then everything was terrible
we scrambled in the middle of the night to borrow a car
drove in silence to hamilton

at that point we weren't sure if we were rushing to see
our little mom with tubes up her nose
        and a sore chest
                and cry it out and then drive back to toronto
or if we she would just be dead
i'd kiss her husk on the forehead and fake emotionless
so that i could
be the scaffolding for a broken sibling

she was alive and her friend was nice and worried and waited
for us to get there before going to find a motel to crash at
with her sister
i started thinking about who i would be more sad to lose
my mom or dad
that's no fun but it's real
her heart has been through some shit
she has the worst taste in men
my dad included
that night she was definitely winning the horrible contest
that my brain was hosting

that was the second time i'd been to hamilton
the first time was to do a poetry reading and as i was leaving
i heard some gross dude on the street successfully pick up a
girl with the line
    hey crystal, got a light? got any rock? wanna fuck?
and she said yup and they headed into an alleyway
that's what hamilton is in a nutshell
moms on the verge of death
sad kids and crackheads having sex in public

DOLPH LUNDGREN COULD HAVE BEEN A SCIENTIST,
BUT HE CHOSE TO BE A GOD

this brain runs
this brain is in way better shape that the rest of its shell
a totally shredded krang from the ninja turtles
perched in the belly of jabba the hutt

at three in the morning
this brain runs
almost like clock work
the schedule and routine of a residual haunting
this brain is screaming drunk in the streets
this brain is being removed from a sports game
has its friends tell them that they should look into getting help
            gets embarrassed
                        gets mad
gets the sense that they're right so it stops talking to them
out of sight of mind
out of brain out of hand

this brain panics and hides from its thirty-first birthday like
it's dimming the lights as the debt collector pounds on the
front door
this brain feels the eyes of its biological clock
            of its paternal instincts
searing a hole in it
feels that urge to settle down and start a family breathing
down its neck
            no romance
            all murder
should be more like the movies
shouldn't make you go balder faster
hope you'll be as good of a parent as you know your partner
will be
this brain gets heart burn and heart broken

night sweats fuel the grease fire
drown this brain
this brain swims with its shirt on
     once a poor fat kid with a lisp
        always a poor fat kid with a lisp
this is all fact no matter what the brain learns

the inside of the skull is
detroit after dark
the file for bankruptcy detroit
not the motown detroit
this detroit looks longingly towards windsor
imagining what could have been
     and windsor isn't even that great
this is detroit with its
automotive plants wilting
this is detroit the lonely and left behind
no lights in some neighborhoods
no cops where they're needed
just the ghost of robocop
     wandering aimlessly
checking the pulse of his flashing 12:00
this prolonged detroit themed metaphor is proof that this brain
is out of control

ACTIVATE NOW

i hope i'm doing better in some other dimension
i hope i got my shit together on the other side
of the wormhole
i hope the other side of the looking glass ain't asking
if there are any beds at the shelter
polishing itself with a pot leaf bandana

i was born in a small town and will die in a big bang
flash of light
strobes from my tongue
disco ball fillings
a heart that'll cause photokeratitis
mobbing an empty notebook
fill it with
words like a *teddy ruxpin*
watch it unfold all on its own
        ghosts in the laundry room
let the lead squirm like a human centipede
weak in the knees
this shit just pours out
the culmination
of being sick with frustration
at a job that requires zero concentration
and once i'm done counting my tips i feel so beat down
i just wanna go home and
david carradine myself
pump it like a shotgun until
love kills me like kurt cobain
and all we're left with
is a well worn plaid shirt
tied like a tourniquet
around our wastes
so our garbage never strays too far

we're so introverted we make like kamala
and swallow the night sky
        moon in our guts
and build star charts in our breasts
sentences spilling out
soak our faces
in crimson honesty
abdullah the butcher
fumbling over words like george steel with
        an emerald mouth full of turnbuckle
all our cries for help sound like
egyptian reggae on a toy piano
a moshpit of wind chimes
teeth click like baseball cards in bike spokes

i'm trying to figure out how a re-roll works in real life
my d-twenty tattoo spins like a cd at a strip club
as a dancer does one last routine
so that she can afford to pick up extra school supplies for her
kids on her way home
you've been in a slump
and it's hard to get back into
the swing of things
when everything makes you dizzy
i'm digging a mass grave in my backyard
and telling my neighbours it's gonna be a pool

this is a call to arms for us
        us
trust us to bust with machine gun pacing
and death metal syllables.
us nice guys who listen to scary music

us who were raised working class and in government housing
but are able to recognize that to some
      we lived like kings
us who die daily
      frenzied flailing
fighting back the frost giants
us guys who suck in our stomachs
us girls who hate our thighs and butts
us who wanna meet a rad girl or guy
take them back to our place
get real close
and then talk all night
until our voices sound like we sing in death metal bands
and our hearts scrape their knees on the gravel in our words
and it's worth it
      it's always worth it
us overwhelmed by the zombie horde
us working dead end jobs
as we wait for a dream life to come true
even if mister sandman has yet to reveal what that is
us who only
wanna get real jobs because we're starting to get
that special tingling in our hearts balls
that signifies that we wanna start a family
and we don't feel comfortable
trying to raise our seeds as waiters
or cooks or bartenders
or whatever it is that you do to live the life that you lead
us with emotional spanks on
us who can forget how much good there is out there
and the cute babies and kind strangers that snap us out
of being turbo goths

us who front hard but
get choked up over the simplest things
us who can see the beauty in repetition
us who tangle our tongues into figure eights
and invite the infinite realities of others to get caught
in our throats
as quinn mallory from tv's *sliders* pushes past us
and checks for the squeaky gate he grew up with
unaware that it had just been oiled
and that this is as good as it gets

Look At My Muscles

today should be a good day
as long as i don't happen to walk past any reflective surfaces
or hear an audio recording of my voice
or watch a video recording of my face
or look at my hairline while i'm brushing my teeth
or focus on the amount of blood i spit out
when i brush my teeth
or happen to look at the mirror to check out my outfit for
the day
or have anyone mention my posture
or try to stand up straight
        shoulders back
only to give up after about thirty seconds when gravity
force-feeds me a mind eraser
or think about money
or consider buying lunch
or get winded after riding my bike for two blocks
or go to the gym and see a bunch of people in better shape
than me
or feel shitty when i eat a deep and delicious cake for lunch
        a whole cake
                or sweat when i eat that cake
or it rains or is too hot or too cold or too windy

today should be a good day
as long as i don't have to be social at any point
as long as i can block out the anxiety
as long as everything i eat doesn't give me heartburn
or make me have to go to the bathroom immediately
no matter what i eat
no matter where i am
as long as i don't think about the relationship i have
with my dad

as long as i don't think about the relationship
my future son could one day have with me
and that relationship is shitty and bad and i'm a bad father
as long as i don't think about my writing
and all the failures anyone who pursues any sort of creative art
faces on a near constant basis
and i can't think of the successes
because they're always hanging out with the failures
and i wish they weren't so close
        success needs to get better friends
i wish they weren't siamese twins
i wish i had used a term other than siamese twin
because that sounds definitely racist
like saying i feel like i got *gypped* in the genetic lottery
like i have the body of a melting uncle phil statue
made out of wax the colour of a baby pig
like i'm always clearing my throat
always worried that i have nothing to say
or that when i do i'll stutter and get embarrassed and mad
always worried
3c-po with golden bones encased in the body
of a sketchy drifter
or a pervert
or a loser
who wishes he was a role model
or a millionaire
wishes he was whatever he isn't
the grass is always greener when landscaping companies rely
so heavily on shamrock coloured spray paint and suspension
of disbelief

today should be a good day as long
as it doesn't get measurably worse
as long as my circuits don't fry
and my eyes spring a leak in public
today should be a good day
i remind myself over and over again
today should be a good day

XEROX ME, JESUS

i'm of the school of thought
that ghosts are psychic stains
left behind long after someone has died
ghosts are a video looped for what could be eternity
of an action that someone undertook frequently when they
were still alive
for example
if someone sees or hears the ghost of a woman
walk up and down a certain flight of stairs
everyday at noon
i would say that when she was alive
that woman probably walked up and down those stairs at noon
nearly everyday
and what you're seeing is the energy she left behind
ghosts are gods photocopies
think of this as a more elaborate adaptation of
what happens when you press a sweaty palm against glass
            you leave the imprint there momentarily
people can now high five you from afar

this has me wondering if
in the future
instead of our grandchildren hearing us shuffle along corridors
they'll hear the tap tap tapping
of a phantom keyboard
the sudden eerie and inexplicable illumination
coming from their closet,
reminiscent of glow bugs stuffed in mason jars
            fireflies are shooting stars in the palm of your hand
simply the halcyon echo of a poltergeist's cellphone

If It's Not Underwater

my mother
truly honestly believes
that if a groundhog
      somewhere in middle america,
surrounded by bill murray memorabilia
sees its shadow
it'll affect global weather patterns
if this was 400 years ago
terrified villagers would be filling her pockets with stones
      tossing her into a river to see if she sinks or swims
before that men were hung in france for being too teen wolf
for comfort

when i grow dead
i wanna be just like my mom
      but these are modern times
i hope the townsfolk chase me through the concrete moors
of toronto's west end
with digital pitchforks and ed hardy zippos
accused by a jealous neighbour of being a mecha godzilla
burnt at the steak like i'm ed -209 from robocop
my kin are a coven of borgs
      yeah
that'd be a cool way to go
my power glove lungs trump your outdated wizards
let the priests
melt my chips down
like a candy bar in the july eyes of an overripe fat kid

I Bought a New Shirt For This

a lot of people brought babies to the funeral
the priest was ok
i don't usually like the god bullies that work these things
this guy wasn't bad
i'm not saying i want him at my funeral when i die
but i think dave would have been alright with this
        dave is the ashes in the box with the photographs
an old leather biker jacket behind it
the ashes in the box used to be a tough guy with a bushy
handle-bar moustache
he was my old man's eldest brother
and after thirty odd years the junk caught up with him
carved *hepatitis* into his back
with a syringe shaped like a switchblade
that just missed his lungs
now he's light grey in a wooden box stained the colour of
fancy floors
as a bagpiper that we paid to be here waits in the wings and
fixes his kilt

the saddest parts are the eulogies that two of his kids deliver
while the other two kids
the ones that live three provinces east of here and were all but
completely ignored for most of their lives
sit in the front row and watch them like a sad movie that
they snuck into
they all have the same jaw line
and it's shaking in unison

my sister is crying to the left of me so i put an arm around her
lasso her close
i'm attempting to comfort us both
while looking like i'm strong

hours from now we will be in an argument that
climaxes with the all seeing fuck you's that refuse
to look at each other
then head back to the city on separate buses
we won't speak for the longest days that april knows
until we run into each other in public
and the tide takes our eyes
and we wonder what just happened here

my cousin michael sits to my right
        plays with his car keys
when he mumbles the responses that the catholic priest
asks for he sounds italian because he was raised by his fathers
immigrant parents
he always looks tired and bummed out
he's one of my favourite people in the room
he talks slowly
and likes betting on horse races

other than the rainy day christians echoing the priest
in their sloppy attempts at avoiding hellfire
all is silent
        no one talks out of turn
cooing infants chirp like crickets
diapered coyotes with cow licks and shiny shoes
serenade one another from the
balcony of their parent's lap
in the name of the father
the son
and my dead uncle's holy ghost
amen

Cleaning People In Love

when i die
i want grave robbers to peel back the lid to my coffin
like the dog eared page of their favorite book
their eyes will be snow globes
my mouth is a pillow fort
i use to cushion lies
i hide behind my lips like a boarded up window
my mouth is a recycling plant
my heart is the fantasized tickle fight at a sorority house
my heart is the line up for a roller coaster
that will inevitably make me sick to my stomach
my guts are psychic
my actions pretend they can speak to the dead
        selling fortunes for fortunes
i crack smiles like fortune cookies and hope for the best

the whites of your eyes afford me the rotating reassurance
of a light house
my pupils are the peepholes of a sinking ship
my arms are the wingspan of a ostrich
        let me embrace you with my uselessness
or i can lie on my back and balance your hips on my feet
and blow until i'm blue in the face to simulate the jet
streams you deserve
        jets streams that hug your curves like all season tires
and we waltz like professional wrestlers
as you try to read my goose bumps like braille

my spine is broken
my spine is the bracket encompassing all thoughts
concerning my low self-esteem
as it reaches for its twin

i was raised on the notion that breath is the purest sound
so when i'm lonely i stick my head in the freezer
    sigh
    and make believe i'm chatting with the ghost
    of a my grandmother

my moustache never fully developed
my eyebrows are telling secrets
my hair line is a mink yarmulke
    my hair is thinning like the competition in the final
round of a beauty pageant
my knees crack like mob snitches
my hands are granite in december

sometimes i wish raptors still existed
so i could get disemboweled and finally spill my guts to
somebody
my dreams are a new born baby with a full head of hair
my dreams are lifelike
my dna strands are broken slinkys
my dick has scene a thousand deaths and lived to tell the tale
some of my memories are actually stowaway scenes
from movies
    satellites mistaken for shooting stars
wish all you want
but nasa doesn't grant new bmx's or more white blood cells

my eyes dart like poison arrows
    shift in their seats like suicide bombers
    having second thoughts
my favorite piece of literature is attempting to read
my own facial expressions

through a shower steamed mirror
i'm more self-centered than zero-gravity
i'm six feet three inches past the womb
and when i left i took the towels and the housecoats with me
      refused to pay for them
and now they wont let me back in

Time's Up, Dummy

i don't care about going bald
i look good with a shaved head
i look tougher
or stronger
or thinner
or rugged
i look like i'm dying
          does it look like i have cancer
i have tons of white blood cells
          maybe too many
i have a beard and that hair didn't fall out
that ain't right
i don't have cancer

          do i look like a nazi
i'm big with tattoos and a shaved head
and i wear combat boots a lot
and
oh god people are gonna think i'm a nazi
i need to hang out with less white people if i'm gonna shave
my head or get a bunch of bob marley shirts
or always tell people how much i relate
to ahbed from community
          or always say i'm craving sushi when people ask
          if i'm hungry
i don't care if i'm losing my hair a little
it's no big deal
it's not that bad
i don't need to shave it all off just yet
i'll keep my hair until it's really obvious
          it's really obvious
i used to have such thick amazing curly hair
i still do have that hair

just not at the front
i'm lucky i'm so tall
so people cant look down at me and the thin zone
i could get a big tattoo on my head
like bam bam bigelow
everybody loved bam bam bigelow
let's be honest
          i'm no bam bam bigelow
it's time i finally came to terms with that

i have dad head
zany uncle head
stressed out nerd
do i grow out the cowlick and slick it over head
i'm gonna have a horse shoe of baldness
everyone sees it
and looks at my hairline when they talk to me
i'll just wear hats
          all of the time
i will never take my hat off

does this mean i have to get a real job even sooner
          bald guys look older than guys with a good hairdo
i'm gonna look like a down on his luck fifty year old man
waiting tables no one will tip me unless it's to say
          hey, i have a tip for you get a real job or stop looking
like a lonely pervert
i'm too young to go bald
          right

i'm thirty
fuck i'm thirty
i'm getting old
i don't have the same head of hair that i had when i was
eighteen
and that means i'm gonna die soon
      and that's science

Too Soft; Broke

i am both the obese sullen southern pageant mom
looking to live out her
dream of being a babe
through the generous people at
the jon benet ramsey make a wish foundation
and the over-competitive
eight year old girl
trying to scream her way out of her
southern wear outfit
          tearing it open like a water damaged paper back
a pretty little hulk hogan,
complete with spray on tan and silky white hair
at war with her tiny yellow emotional tank top

i feel like i'm always holding my tongue
lips locked like opposing halves of
a george foreman grill
intersecting crocodile teeth
          locked hands
with fingers like plaid
with fingers like kerplunk rods
over lapping, french braid shoelace digits
          let it build up
until my mouth bursts open
an over done pizza pocket

and that's the story of my life
i always over do things
i'm old enough to recognize how ridiculous i get
know that i'm too old to blame my disasters on drop dead fred
          feel like i look like rick from the young ones
i'm joey gladstone in the back of a squad car on cops
          banging his head against the window

in a vomit covered america's funniest people t-shirt
as if the concussion he's giving himself
is the punch line to the greatest knock-knock joke
he'll ever write

this is the blasphemy of over-reaction
of not being able to sleep
of staring at a five year plan like it was a firing squad
        don't shoot until you can't see
        through the snowstorms of their eyes
        the blizzard eclipsing the pin pricks of black out
        white paint splashed over spent match heads

i'm a narcoleptic edgar casey
day dreaming of a better tomorrow as sleep let's slip secrets of
doomsdays and disasters
i'm pee wee herman being patched into the hell's angels
        braver than john goodman in *arachnophobia*
with nausea like my instincts and lactose intolerance are
working in tandem
to guide me to a safety
i have all of the direction of a bike
with tires trapped in streetcar tracks
        head straight until you decide change is needed
        at which point
        fall over and get hit and murdered by a car

all i want to do is meet a nice jewish or jew-ish girl
and settle down
        but i'm in love with the terrifying beauty of the hustle
all of my dreams are steam punks on acid
my best dreams stick around while i go about my day to day
        but none of my dreams are worth talking about

too many of my friends are friends with needles
all of my friends are like my best comic books
       today they're great but they'll be worth even more
       if i keep them in good condition
       down the road
none of my friends care about punctuation
all of my poems are the world's most powerful wizard
with a spell casting inhibiting stutter and severe agoraphobia
all of my poems will see you in valhalla
none of these words like each other
these words erode the person and expose the panic
these tools only work to deconstruct
these past lives wanna stay retired
these reincarnations
don't know when enough is enough
these regrets are that guy from *memento*
this is waking up early
       staring at the dead bodies in front of it
          the blood on its hands
this is thinking how weird it is that these days
real life things can be so real they look fake
star-wipe away the gore
fade to black
this isn't the end
being swallowed by the leviathan
this isn't the pearly gates with a sign stuck to it that says
       please use the other door
this is the pop and lock of a bell tower sniper
my cheeks burn like mix cds in high school
       and old churches in norway
i put everything on the line
hang my inner demons out to dry

in hopes that somebody
        anybody
comes up to me
when all is said and done
and tells me that they can relate to what i'm going through
a spoon full of sugar
makes me feel more normal
        make it less lonely
                makes it all makes sense
my body is science
my heart a bunsen burner
a child's chemistry set
collects dust behind sparse chest hair
while the anarchist's cookbook stays steadily lodged
in my windpipes
i pull my hair out like it's unconscious in a burning car
grinding my teeth like a creep in a nightclub
        the mortar and pestle bang like make-up sex
this isn't hell on earth
don't be such a drama queen
this is just heaven with the basement flooded
the eye of providence with conjunctivitis
this is the arthritic hand of god
signing that it can't keep picking me back up
because it's afraid that i'll shatter in its cumulonimbus grip

Acknowledgements

This book would not have been possible without the help and support of my family and friends. Special thanks to my mom, my sister Kerry, my wife Stephanie, The Weinz family, The Toronto Poetry Slam crew, Hypertrophic Literary, The Sophisticated Boom Boom Poetry Series, Blue Coffee Reading Series, The Vancouver Poetry Slam crew, The Talkhole Podcast Network and AMAZING THINGS crew, Daniel/Pearl Harbor Gift Shop Tattoos for helping me scrap book, all of my friends who I bounce writing ideas off of and will continue to do so whether they like it or not, Chris and Now Or Never Publishing for being patient and YOU for buying (and hopefully liking) this book.

HIGH PEAKS ENGINEERING

Rocky Mountain Marvels

L.D. CROSS

VICTORIA · VANCOUVER · CALGARY

Heritage House Publishing Company Ltd.
heritagehouse.ca

Library and Archives Canada Cataloguing in Publication
Cross, L. D. (L. Dyan), 1949-, author
High peaks engineering : Rocky Mountain marvels / L.D. Cross.

(Amazing stories)
Issued in print and electronic formats.
ISBN 978-1-927527-80-1 (pbk.).—ISBN 978-1-927527-81-8 (html).—ISBN 978-1-927527-82-5 (pdf)

1. Engineering—Rocky Mountains, Canadian (B.C. and Alta.)—History. 2. Rocky Mountains, Canadian (B.C. and Alta.)—History. I. Series: Amazing stories (Victoria, B.C.)

TA27.R6 C76 2014   364.1092'2   C2013-908571-8   C2013-908572-6

Edited by Leslie Kenny
Proofread by Vivian Sinclair

Cover photo: Canadian Pacific Railway train approaching the Lower Spiral Tunnel near Field, British Columbia, *circa* 1940. Glenbow Archives NA-3194-8.

The interior of this book was produced on 30% post-consumer recycled paper, processed chlorine free and printed with vegetable-based inks.

Heritage House acknowledges the financial support for its publishing program from the Government of Canada through the Canada Book Fund (CBF), Canada Council for the Arts, and the Province of British Columbia through the British Columbia Arts Council and the Book Publishing Tax Credit.

 Canadian Heritage Patrimoine canadien   Canada Council for the Arts Conseil des Arts du Canada   BRITISH COLUMBIA ARTS COUNCIL Supported by the Province of British Columbia

18 17 16 15 14   1 2 3 4 5
Printed in Canada